GOING BACK HOME

AN ARTIST RETURNS TO THE SOUTH

PICTURES BY MICHELE WOOD

STORY INTERPRETED AND WRITTEN BY TOYOMI IGUS

CHILDREN'S BOOK PRESS

SAN FRANCISCO, CALIFORNIA

When I was a little girl, I heard many stories about my family—where they came from, what life was like before I was born. This is a picture of me sitting at my aunt's knee, listening to her tales as she did my hair.

Of course, I didn't grow up in a house like this. I grew up in a big city in Indiana. But I tried to imagine what kind of house my ancestors lived in when they were enslaved on a plantation in the South. I thought it might look something like this.

I was fascinated by my family's stories. I was the curious one who would listen to the grownups' tales. As I grew older, I tried to piece together my family's history from the scraps of memories they would share with me. When you look at my art, you will see that I often create quilt-like backgrounds. This is my way of showing how pieces of life can fit together.

Because I am an artist, I express my thoughts and feelings visually, through pictures. This picture, "The Family Way," represents family love and togetherness. When I set out to trace my family tree, my family supported me in every way.

I call this picture "Inheritors of Slavery" to represent the many generations of my people who were enslaved. The woman is holding a black pot, which she used in Africa and here in her new homeland. It symbolizes family and the continuation of our heritage. Behind the couple, you can see symbols of their life in America: the well, from which they drew their water; the wash tub and scrub board, which they used to clean their clothes; the hen, which provided food for people here and in Africa; and the little house they were given by their masters to live in. The hen and the house are powerful symbols for me. I use them a lot in my artwork.

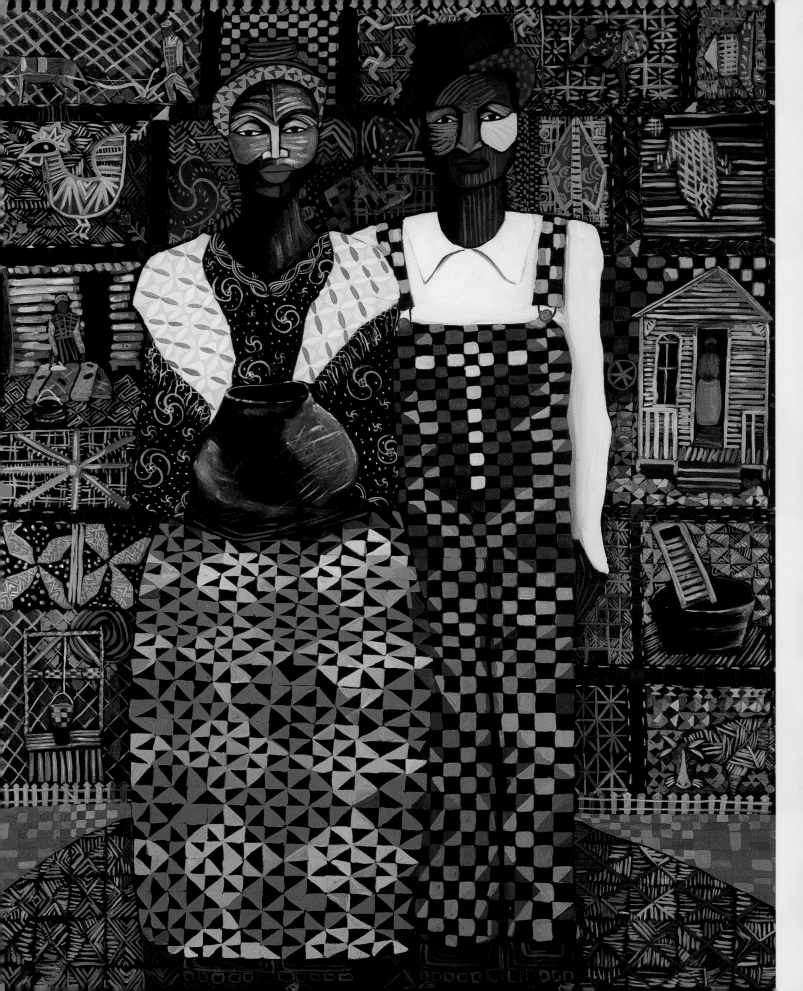

When I got older, I had a strong desire to go back home to the South to actually see and feel the land where my ancestors lived. So I left Indiana, moved to Atlanta, Georgia, and started exploring the southern United States. I visited plantations and read a lot about the history of African Americans.

I once saw a picture of a doll that a little slave girl named Emmaline made for her white master's daughter. I felt sad when I thought about the doll that Emmaline could not own, so I painted this picture. I dressed the doll in red, white, and blue to represent America. Behind her you can see an African American soldier who fought for this country even though our people were not allowed to be free here.

Both my mother's and father's families were from the Mississippi Delta. After the Civil War, my family, like many former slaves, did not leave the South right away. Instead they stayed and sharecropped. Sharecropping was a method of farming where poor farmers had to borrow land to farm—and also tools and seed. The crop they grew went to pay off their debts.

This picture of my great-grandparents is similar to "Inheritors of Slavery," two scenes ago. But I painted the couple standing *inside* their house to show the wonderful possibility they now had of making their own home. The pinwheels on the woman's skirt are ancient symbols that stand for good luck and the changing cycles of life. The mule in the man's hands represents the "forty acres and a mule" that were promised—but never delivered—to the freed slaves.

My family grew cotton. From dawn to dusk, everyone on the farm had to work. The women looked after the children, picked the cotton during harvest time, tended the livestock, and planted the family vegetable garden. The men plowed and weeded the fields day after day and hunted 'possums, 'coons, and deer for food.

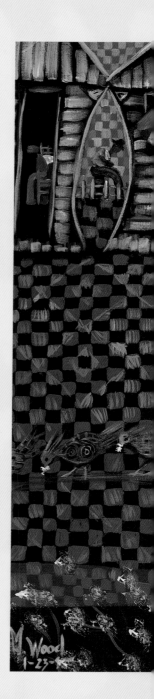

In this picture you can see how the women would pick cotton and put it in their aprons. As their aprons filled up, the women—and children too—would drag their load behind them as they picked the bits of fluff. Slaves had picked cotton the very same way one hundred years before. It was a very hard life. If you look closely, you can see that I even made the hens work!

In those days, families depended a lot more on each other. Survival demanded that people work together in harmony—like the man and the woman in this picture.

Water was important too. It was the source of life—for my family, for their livestock, for the crops. This is why I made the well the central image in this painting. The wheel on the well is there to bring good fortune. Behind the couple I painted bottle trees. People believed that bottle trees brought rain.

I wanted this picture to say that with hard work, a little luck, and a strong community, my family was able to thrive even under the harshest of conditions.

usic has always been an important part of African American culture. Slaves sang work songs to make their hard work easier and used field hollers—long, drawn out notes—to express emotion and warn each other of danger. From these songs and religious spirituals came the blues.

American music has been greatly influenced by the blues. Important blues songs and singers came from the Mississippi Delta where my family lived. As I traveled around the South, I would often see scenes like this—men sitting on the front stoop playing the guitar or harmonica and singing the blues. It was easy for me to imagine my own great-grandfather easing out of his tiresome day by making some music.

Despite the hard work, or maybe because of it, families took every opportunity to celebrate life. Births, weddings, harvest time, baptisms— then, as now, families rejoiced in the good times. The women would prepare for days, cooking and baking, using the precious white sugar and white flour to create the confections reserved for such occasions.

Whenever I think of my foremothers cooking for special days, I see this picture of my grandmother Kathryn and remember how she used to bake a treat for each family member on every holiday.

Do you see the snails on her dress? I copied the pattern from one of my favorite Nigerian outfits. My grandmother didn't really have a dress like this, but I liked it, so I gave the dress to her in this picture.

I call this painting "The Wedding Dance to Happiness." The women in my family didn't have fancy wedding dresses, just their usual cotton frocks. But even though the fabric was simple, they would make the dresses beautiful by using colorful dyes. On a wedding day, the men would get all cleaned up and put on their Sunday best. The preacher might ride out to the farm from a neighboring town to say the wedding vows. Maybe the couple would "jump the broom," which was an old wedding ritual from the slave days that marked the beginning of a couple's new life together. On that special day, all work would stop and the music would flow.

As a child I remember going to churches that were converted old houses, like the one I painted here. After church, folks would always stand outside for a while and talk— about the preacher, about his sermon, about the neighbors, about their kids.

My ancestors probably did the very same thing. Every Sunday after a hard week of farming, they would go to a church like this to socialize and renew their faith. In the South during the early 1900s, the church was often the only safe and welcoming place for African Americans to congregate.

This picture is called "Sunday Morning." I hope it shows how much I respect my elders and their faith in God and in each other.

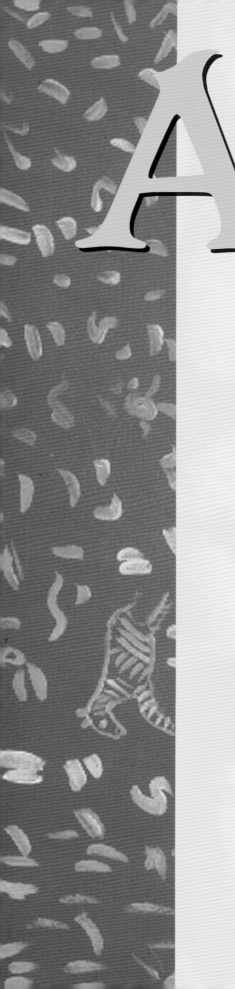

After many years of struggle, it became just too difficult to make a living sharecropping. You never could tell about the cotton crop. If the boll weevils attacked the plants, the harvest would be very poor. If big rains came, the water would flood out the fields. Sharecroppers had to borrow more and more to live, so their debts would grow and grow. Over time many black people, like my family, moved North, where there were now other jobs on the railroads and in the steel mills.

I call this picture "The Wagon to Freedom." I tried to imagine what it was like for my family to leave the land where they had lived for so long and to look—for the last time—at the houses that were the only homes they had ever known.

Of course not everyone went North seeking new opportunities. Many African Americans moved West. Although it's not very well known, black men worked all over the West as cowboys. I didn't realize this until I saw a picture of Nat Love, a famous black cowboy. So I painted him. Doesn't he look proud? Nat Love became an expert roper and shooter and was one of the best cowboys of his time.

If you look very closely, in the background you will see that I have painted little pictures of a storefront and of a soldier. This is to show that African Americans were—and are—very self-sufficient. We owned businesses, fought in all of the American wars, and contributed greatly to the building of this country.

My grandmother Kathryn's branch of the family left Mississippi and moved north to Kentucky, where she was born and raised. For a long time Kathryn never went to fancy restaurants or hotels because black people were not allowed inside. After segregation ended, my grandmother was able to eat in one of these restaurants for the very first time. It must have taken a great deal of courage. I imagine that she looked like this—dignified, with her head held high, but clutching her purse close beside her. Even though she looked proud and courageous, deep down inside she was a little bit scared!

As I learned about my family's history and all that they endured, I realized that I come from a very strong people. I never tried to create a self-portrait before, but after going back home, an image of myself started to form in my mind.

Here it is. I laughed when I painted the square on my forehead. When I was little, I tried to take a picture of myself, and I put the camera too close in front of my face. The flashbulb made a square-shaped burn on my forehead. The mark is gone now, but I remembered it in this picture.

The house and fence represent the foundations of my past. The boards are my life's lessons— the crooked ones are the tragedies and hardships. I am holding a hen, which is the link to my rural southern heritage.

And the woman in the window? She's the person I have yet to become. After going back home, I know more about who I am and I can picture the person I want to be—a seeker of knowledge, a creator of visions, and a keeper of my family's history.

GOING BACK HOME: AN ARTIST RETURNS TO THE SOUTH

The story of *Going Back Home* began with African American artist Michele Wood's magnificent paintings based on her family's history in the southern United States. When Children's Book Press publisher Harriet Rohmer saw the paintings, she thought that they would make an inspiring book for children. Would Michele be willing to work with an experienced African American author who would give words to her story? Michele agreed, and so Harriet asked Toyomi Igus, the Editor and Publications Director of the Center for African American Studies at UCLA to interview Michele and to interpret her visual images and oral histories. *Going Back Home* is the result of this collaborative effort.

MICHELE WOOD is a painter, media artist, and printmaker whose work has gained wide recognition in the United States, Canada, and Nigeria. She was commissioned to create the 1993 Black History Month jazz series poster for the city of Atlanta, and her painting, "Inheritors of Slavery," was selected by the Tubman Museum for presentation to Jesse Jackson. She currently lives and works in Atlanta, Georgia.

TOYOMI IGUS is the Editor and Publications Director at UCLA's Center for African American Studies and the author and editor of several books for children, including *Two Mrs. Gibsons*, also published by Children's Book Press. Her current projects at UCLA include the development of a two-volume publication profiling contemporary African American artists of Southern California.

This book is dedicated to the four special women in my life, Karolyn A. Mitchel, Marchel Hall, Kathryn Taylor, and Marian Langly with immeasurable love. —M.W.

To Darrow and Dad, with love. —T.I.

Pictures copyright © 1996 by Michele Wood. All rights reserved.
Story copyright © 1996 by Toyomi Igus. All rights reserved.
Editors: Harriet Rohmer and David Schecter
Design and Production: John Miller, Big Fish
Editorial/Production Assistant: Laura Atkins

Thanks to the staff of Children's Book Press: Jenny Brandt, Andrea Durham, Janet Levin, Emily Romero, and Stephanie Sloan.

Children's Book Press is a nonprofit publisher of multicultural literature for children, supported in part by grants from the California Arts Council.
Write us for a complimentary catalog:
Children's Book Press, 246 First Street, Suite 101, San Francisco, CA 94105

Library of Congress Cataloging-in-Publication Data
Going back home: an artist returns to the South/pictures by Michele Wood; interpreted and written by Toyomi Igus. p. cm.
Summary: Narrative text describes the artist's paintings and their portrayal of the lives of her African American relatives in the rural American South. ISBN 0-89239-137-5
1. Wood, Michele—Juvenile literature. 2. Afro-American painters—Biography—Juvenile literature. 3. Afro-Americans in art—Juvenile literature. 4. Afro-Americans—Southern States—Juvenile literature. [1. Wood, Michele. 2. Artists. 3. Afro-Americans—Biography. 4. Women—Biography. 5. Southern States—Social life and customs. 6. Art appreciation.] I. Igus, Toyomi. II. Title.
ND237.W796W66 1995 759.13—dc20 96-7458 CIP AC

Printed in Hong Kong through Marwin Productions
10 9 8 7 6 5 4 3 2 1

Grandma Moses

written and illustrated by
ALEXANDRA WALLNER

HOLIDAY HOUSE / New York

For their help, my thanks go to:

Stephen Perkins
Curator of the Bennington Museum
Bennington, Vermont

Joyce St. Jacques
Member of the Historical Committee
Washington County Fair Grounds Museum
Greenwich, New York

Copyright © 2004 by Alexandra Wallner
All Rights Reserved
Printed in the United States of America
www.holidayhouse.com
First Edition
1 3 5 7 9 10 8 6 4 2

Library of Congress Cataloging-in-Publication Data
Wallner, Alexandra.
Grandma Moses / written and illustrated by Alexandra Wallner—1st ed.
p. cm.
Summary: A brief biography of Anna Mary Robertson, the artist who was known as Grandma Moses,
describing the inspiration behind and development of her paintings.
ISBN 0-8234-1538-4 (hardcover)
1. Moses, Grandma, 1860-1961—Juvenile literature.
2. Painters—United States—Biography—Juvenile literature.
[1. Moses, Grandma, 1860-1961. 2. Artists. 3. Women—Biography.
4. Painting, American.] I. Title.
ND237.M78W35 2004
759.13—dc21
[B]
2003050919

"If I didn't start painting. I would have raised chickens."
Grandma Moses

*A*nna Mary Robertson was born on September 7, 1860, on a farm in Washington County, New York.

She had a happy childhood. During lazy summer days, she floated along the millpond, looking at puffy white clouds on a raft her brothers had built. She ran through fields dotted with sweet-scented wildflowers. Her favorite game, however, was "building air-castles," as she called making believe.

Anna Mary had few toys, so she made her own. Once she cut out paper dolls from newspapers. She painted eyes with blue laundry rinse and lips with grape juice. Her mother's old petticoats made nice "trimmens" for the dolls' dresses. Anna Mary was proud of her first artwork.

One winter her pa got sick. He could not work outdoors.
So he asked Ma if he could paint pictures on the living-room
walls. Ma said she didn't care as long as she got clean walls.

For hours Anna Mary watched Pa paint a scene of nearby
Lake George. When he was done, Ma was so pleased that she
asked Pa to paint the whole room full of outdoor scenes, or
"landscapes."

Making pictures looked like fun to Anna Mary, so she painted scenes of hills, lakes, fields, and trees on pieces of slate and windowpanes. She called them her "very pretty *lamb* scapes," which made her brother laugh.

Pa liked Anna Mary's paintings, but Ma needed her to help with farmwork.

In winter Anna Mary carried buckets of maple sap for making syrup. She helped Ma mold candles and soap. She did housework and helped neighbors, too. There was little time for school, three months in summer and three in winter. Certainly, there was no time at all for painting pictures.

When Anna Mary was twelve, she left home to work as a hired girl. She worked hard for a nearby family, cooking three meals a day, tending a large garden, washing, ironing, and churning butter. After a few years she worked for another family, who let her go to school when chores were done.

In school she sometimes was allowed to draw. She enjoyed making maps. Her teacher asked if he could have one, because he liked the way she drew mountains. She was pleased that someone liked her artwork.

In autumn 1886, when Anna Mary was a young woman, she went to work for another family. There she met Thomas Salomon Moses, a hired man. Anna Mary got to know and respect Thomas. She later wrote, "In those days we didn't look for a man with money, but for a good family, good reputation — many of the boys were chicken thieves . . ."

Anna Mary and Thomas loved each other, and a year later they got married. Then they moved near Staunton, Virginia, in the Shenandoah valley to manage a dairy farm. They bought two cows on credit. While churning milk into butter, Anna Mary sat on the porch and watched the landscape. The setting sun changed green hills to blue. A train's gray smoke curled into the pink sky. How she wished she had time to paint the scene! Instead she turned a lot of milk into butter and proudly paid for the cows.

Soon Anna Mary had a baby and the family moved to Mt. Airy Farm. She had nine more babies, but not all lived. "... five little graves I left in that beautiful Shenandoah valley," she sadly wrote.

The family eventually moved back to New York. They bought a dairy farm near Eagle Bridge, which they called Mt. Nebo.

Anna Mary spent her days cooking, washing, ironing, mending, gardening, feeding chickens, and raising children. One day she was wallpapering the parlor and ran out of paper. Still yearning to make pictures, she saw a chance. She painted two large trees on either side of the fireboard, and in the middle she painted a lake with big bushes. Her family admired the scene.

"That was my first large picture," she later wrote.

Her children grew up and left home, but still Anna Mary was busy helping Thomas run the farm. They found time for fun, though, going to church, on picnics, or on buggy rides. She watched people skating on ponds in winter and children flying kites in spring. Anna Mary treasured these wonderful memories. Perhaps someday she would have time to make them into pictures.

In the very cold January of 1927, Thomas got sick and died suddenly. With her children gone and her husband dead, Anna Mary was lonely for the first time in her life. But now she had time for her artwork. When she turned to it, she found it comforting. Finally she could show people the many happy memories she had gathered over a lifetime, and they could see the world through her eyes.

She made many "worsted pictures" with brightly colored yarns. When her fingers developed rheumatism and she could no longer hold a needle, she turned to painting.

Anna Mary often felt Thomas was watching over her shoulder and whispering to her what to paint. She wrote, "I never know how I'm going to paint until I start in; something tells me what to go right on and do."

For the next ten years Anna Mary painted many scenes. ". . . always something pleasing and cheerful. I like bright colors and activity," she wrote.

Anna Mary used cheap paint and brushes. She used toothpicks for fine details and glitter on snow scenes to make them sparkle.

In 1938, after painting a lot of pictures, she decided to exhibit some of them in the Hoosick Falls drugstore.

"I also exhibited a few at the Cambridge Fair with some canned fruits and raspberry jam," she wrote. "I won a prize for my fruit and jam, but no pictures."

She was disappointed, but didn't let it stop her. She was having too much fun.

One day an art collector from New York, Louis Caldor, passed through Hoosick Falls and saw Anna Mary's pictures. He liked her scenes of farm life and of days gone by. He said the cozy pictures made him feel happy and he thought other people would feel the same way.

Louis Caldor took the pictures to New York. He said an art gallery there might want to show them.

Months went by, but none of the galleries were interested. Although the art dealers liked the pictures, they didn't want to take a chance on an unknown artist who was close to eighty years old.

When the Museum of Modern Art had an exhibit of unknown American painters, three of her paintings were shown.

Then, in 1940, the Galerie St. Etienne said it would display her pictures.

People liked the honest way Anna Mary painted memories from her heart. They smiled at scenes of long-ago days— quilting bees, playing in the snow, families getting together on holidays. Through her pictures, they felt as if they knew her. She was like their own grandmother. Soon Anna Mary came to be known as Grandma Moses.

"When my exhibition opened, large numbers of elderly people came, having heard my story," she wrote.

Old people said they were inspired by her example. They admired her for starting a new career at her age.

Her pictures were reproduced on greeting cards, and soon many people knew Grandma's artwork.

In 1949 President Harry S Truman presented her with the Women's National Press Club Award, "for outstanding accomplishment in art."

She was interviewed on radio and TV.

Asked about how she painted, Grandma answered, "Before I started painting, I get a frame, then I saw my Masonite board to fit the frame. (I always thought it a good idea to build the sty before getting the pig. . . .)"

She also modestly wrote, "I am doing better work than at first, but it is owing to better brushes and paint."

People paid her a lot of money for her artwork, but that didn't matter to her.

Grandma was now a famous artist. She remembered a dream her father had about her when she was a little girl.

"He dreamed I was in a large hall and there were many people there, they were clapping their hands and shouting and he wondered what it was all about," she wrote.

She was glad that she finally had a chance to make pictures and that people enjoyed the pretty world she created. Grandma Moses died on December 13, 1961, at the age of 101.

She had once said, ". . . life is what we make it, always has been, always will be."

Author's Note

During Grandma Moses's life (1860–1961), many things changed in the United States.

When Grandma was a child, people still rode horses, and traveled in wagons, carriages, buggies, and steam-powered trains when they wanted to go someplace. Children often went to one-room schoolhouses, just as Grandma did.

The best fun country people enjoyed was going to country fairs. Grandma looked forward to going all year.

There were nineteen presidents during Grandma's lifetime. She was five years old when President Lincoln was shot. In 1956, after she was famous, she painted President Eisenhower's house as a present to him. President Kennedy sent her a birthday note in 1961.

Governor Rockefeller of New York proclaimed September 7, 1960, Grandma Moses Day.

When she was old, Grandma rode in cars, talked on the telephone, and was interviewed on radio and TV.

Grandma enjoyed painting the changes she saw in the United States as she remembered them. Many of her works can be seen at the Bennington Museum in Bennington, Vermont.

Bibliography

All quotations were taken from
Grandma Moses: My Life's History.

Kallir, Jane. *Grandma Moses, the Artist Behind the Myth.* New York: Clarkson N. Potter, 1982.

Kallir, Otto. *Grandma Moses.* New York: Harry N. Abrams, 1973.

Ketchum, Jr., William C. *Grandma Moses: An American Original.* New York: Todtri Production, Ltd., 1999.

Moses, Anna Mary. Edited by Otto Kallir. *Grandma Moses: My Life's History.* New York: Harper & Brothers, 1952.

Oneal, Zibby. *Grandma Moses: Painter of Rural America (Women of Our Time).* New York: Viking, 1986.